HISTORY & TECHNIQUES OF THE
Great Masters

GOYA

HISTORY & TECHNIQUES OF THE
Great Masters

GOYA

Michael Howard

Eagle
Editions

A QUANTUM BOOK

Published by Eagle Editions Ltd.
11 Heathfield
Royston
Hertfordshire SG8 5BW

ISBN 1-86160-478-5

QUMGOY

This book is produced by
Quantum Publishing Ltd.
6 Blundell Street
London N7 9BH

Printed in China by
Leefung-Asco Printers Ltd.

CONTENTS

THE PAINTINGS

INTRODUCTION

FRANCISCO GOYA
Self-Portrait
1815-16, Prado, Madrid

Since his death in 1828, Goya's art, personality and even his technical and stylistic repertoire have been the subject of much controversy. His mastery of technique attracted the admiration of a wide variety of 19th-century artists, and continues to do so today, but his virtuosity as a painter and printmaker was never used as an end in itself, but always as a means to express the potential of his subject matter. Consequently, many of his images have become for us some of the most powerful in the whole of Western culture, and although his work is rooted firmly in his own historical period, his continued popularity suggests that it has a particular significance for the present age.

Goya's life coincided with one of the most confused and troubled times of modern European history, a period which helped shape the world we live in today. But his perception of this world was always mediated by his inner life. For him the world of dream was as real as that of waking, and his depictions of both realms possess the sense of immediacy, honesty and sincerity that we recognize in the best work of the news photographers or cameramen of modern times — "I saw this" *(yo lo vi)* is the title of one of his most effective prints. But just as photographers study their techniques and plan their compositions, Goya's work was always the result of careful forethought: his *reportage* was far from being direct experience magically translated onto a canvas or copperplate. He has been called the last of the Old Masters and the first of the new; his people, whether aristocrats or plebeians, peasants, beggars or beauties, are indisputably inhabitants of a world that we recognize — individuals unknown to us, but once seen never forgotten. It seems contradictory that this vision that speaks to us so directly should have been the product of a society that butchered humans and animals alike, a society based on hypocrisy and fear — the Spain of the Inquisition.

Although profoundly critical of human behaviour at every level of society, Goya was fully aware of his need to remain outwardly loyal to the state, and there are many contradictions in both his work and his attitudes. The major political and social upheavals through which he lived, as well as his various illnesses, profoundly affected the nature of his art. He produced work for the state, the Church, private patrons and for his own personal needs and pleasures, but these areas are not always as widely separated as one might think: the many different elements of his art overlap and interweave, creating an *oeuvre* of considerable complexity. Among his private patrons was a small circle of influential intellectuals who longed to see their country lose the shackles that tied it to a superstitious and feudal past. Their wish was to introduce the spirit of the Enlightenment initially associated with France and the French Revolution and later personified by the charismatic figure of Napoleon. Much of Goya's mature work was deeply connected with such ideas, indeed it is clear that much of it was intended to function on various levels and to be open to a number of interpretations. This goes some way to explain its continued impact on an audience that is largely ignorant of the circumstances or social patterns that lay behind its production. But this is only one side of Goya's art: it has often been said that if he had died at the age of forty-five he would have been remembered as a talented painter of tapestry designs for the Spanish court, a craftsman with a fertile imagination and a bravura painting style, happy to remain within the bounds that his own social ambitions had set for him.

Early years

Until his mid-forties, when a mysterious illness caused a change of direction, Francisco José de Goya y Lucientes could be described as the epitome of the self-made man, proud of having found his own way in the world by means of his skill and wit. He was born on 30 March, 1746, in the poor agricultural community of Fuen-

DIEGO VELASQUEZ
Las Meninas
1656, Prado, Madrid

During Goya's lifetime this painting was considered to be the most valuable work in the royal collection. Goya was deeply influenced by Velasquez; he was reported as having said that his only masters were Rembrandt, Velasquez and Nature. Echoes of Velasquez's psychological penetration, his ease with paint and his assured mastery of tone and composition recur in Goya's work throughout his career.

seen in many of the churches and palaces of Spain.

In 1763, aged only seventeen, he attempted unsuccessfully to gain a scholarship to the Academy of San Fernando in Madrid. He made a second attempt three years later and was once again refused. There was not a single vote in his favour despite the presence on the committee of another artist from Aragon, Francesco Bayeu, who held the post of court painter to Charles III, King of Spain.

Goya returned to Saragossa and concentrated upon establishing himself as the major painter of the area, carrying out a series of church frescoes. In 1770/1 he made a trip to Italy, the home of the Baroque style, and visited Rome, Naples and Parma, where he saw the frescoes by Correggio, and must have been impressed by the art of the surrounding region. Writers of the 19th century, who did so much to build the popular idea of Goya's life and personality that still prevails today, record him climbing the dome of St Peter's, getting involved in brawls and so on. Whether or not such stories are true, it

detodos, part of the province of Aragon, situated on the high arid plateau of central Spain. His family were not wealthy; his father, who had been a master gilder, died intestate, and the young Goya was left to make his own way in the world. At the age of fourteen he was apprenticed to a local painter, José Luzán y Martinez, who had been a pupil of the Neapolitan Francesco Solimena, one of the last great painters in the Baroque tradition. At Luzán's studio in Saragossa, Goya was trained to work in the grand and assured theatrical style that could then be

FRANCISCO GOYA
Inquisition Tribunal
c 1812-15, Academy of San Fernando, Madrid

The expressions, attitudes and costumes of the participants in this tragic farce reveal the power and terror embodied by the religious courts of the Inquisition. The influence of this religious institution stretched far beyond the confines of the Church to form a living symbol of the brutal and repressive aspects of "Black Spain" — the still feudal country that was Goya's home.

is certain that he did not neglect his professional concerns, and was commended by the Academy at Parma for his "fluent handling." This aspect of Goya's work and his exquisite sense of tone and colour were to become his dominant stylistic hallmarks.

In 1773 Goya married Josefa Bayeu, sister of the fashionable Francesco Bayeu who was himself the protegé of the Neo-Classical painter Antonio-Raphael Mengs, favourite of the king and virtual dictator of the Spanish art scene. Whether this was a shrewd piece of career building or a love match has been a matter of continued speculation. Goya was a man with a huge appetite for the pleasures of life; he loved hunting, attending the popular fiestas and, if we are to believe the legends, he was an active participant in bullfights. In 1774 Mengs, who was among other things director of the royal weaving mills, invited Goya to work under the direction of his brother-in-law at the royal tapestry factory of Santa Barbara in Madrid. The tapestry cartoons were the first works for which he became popularly known, and for almost twenty years between 1775 and 1792 they formed the basis of his professional activity. He produced sixty-three cartoons for the royal household, forty-three of which are now conserved in the Prado, Madrid.

Fame and success

In December 1778 Goya sent his childhood friend, the intellectual Martín Zapater, eighteen etchings which he had made after the paintings by Velasquez in the royal collection, and in 1780 he was unanimously elected to the Academy of San Fernando on the strength of a deliberately conventionally painted *Crucifixion* closely modelled on a Velasquez painting of the same subject. Goya was later to say that his only teachers had been Velasquez, Rembrandt and nature.

By the 1780s he had a firmly established reputation as a skilled craftsman-artist. In the early years of the decade he had begun to paint society portraits, and these, together with royal commissions and paintings for the Church, continued to be the mainstay of his financial independence. By mid-decade he was free from financial worries and affluent enough to own an expensive English carriage, which he drove so recklessly that he killed a passer-by — he subsequently exchanged this vehicle for a luxurious four-wheeler drawn by two mules.

In 1785 he was appointed deputy director of the Academy, and the next year he became painter to the king *(pintor del rey)*. He was patronized by both the royal

family and the influential and enlightened families of
Spain, and through the patronage of wealthy liberals he
was able to produce more personal works alongside
those in the traditional genres. Religious themes were a
staple of his artistic production — the most profitable in
financial terms — but a large body of his work concerns
the unacceptable face of religion. Subjects such as the
courts of the Inquisition or the activities of witches were
popular with his intellectual friends and patrons, who
saw such themes as metaphors for the fear-ridden state
of their country.

Commissions for tapestry designs also continued, but
Goya's manner of handling them changed considerably,
as may be seen by comparing *A Walk in Andalusia* of 1777
(see page 19) to *Winter,* of ten years later. *Winter* is more
realistic in its treatment of pose, and the effects of atmosphere and weather; it is much more lively and free in
handling and less restricted by the limitations of its
primary purpose — the cartoons took the form of patterns or models to be interpreted by the weavers of the
Santa Barbara factory. By the 1790s Goya's dissatis-
faction with producing these tapestry commissions was

widely known. In April 25 1789, aged forty-three, he was given by Charles IV, who had been crowned King of Spain a few months earlier, the prestigious post of *pintor del cámara del rey*, official painter to the court. He was now at the height of his popularity, and in 1792 he produced his last work for the tapestry factory.

Illness and introspection

1792 was a fateful year for Goya. En route to Cadiz, the seaport on the south west coast of Spain, he became seriously ill. The exact nature of his illness is not known, but it lasted several months, brought him close to death and left him profoundly deaf. Deafness is a disability which separates its victim irretrievably from easy communication with others, and this, together with his narrow escape from death, must have deeply affected Goya's view of himself and his position within society. In January 1794 he submitted eleven paintings for the Academy, and wrote to Bernardo de Iriate, the vice-protector of the Royal Academy in Madrid, that the

pictures presented were executed "...to occupy my imagination, vexed by consideration of my ills, and to ... make observations that normally are given no place in commissioned works which give no scope for fantasy and invention." Such themes were by no means unknown or unique to Goya: in the 17th century Philip II had collected the work of Bosch and Bruegel, both of whom were specialists to varying degrees in the weird and macabre.

Recuperation from his illness kept Goya away from the capital for almost a year, and this period formed the turning point in his work. He became more concerned with developing an art based on his personal interests and began, along with his portraits of the wealthy, to produce new works with an often disturbing subject matter. Simple and dynamic in composition, small in scale, these depicted scenes of natural disaster, gatherings of prisoners, lunatics and witches, episodes of rape, murder, cannibalism and disease.

In 1795 he produced a portrait of the great aristo-

The Naked and Clothed Majas
c 1800, Prado, Madrid

These are two of the most enigmatic images in Western art. They were originally in the Duchess of Alba's own collection, but were subsequently owned by Manuel Godoy, who also possessed Velasquez's so-called *Rokeby Venus*. The nude was extremely rare in Spanish painting, and the unashamed eroticism of these works brought Goya before the Court of the Inquisition.

FRANCISCO GOYA
"The Sleep of Reason Produces Monsters"
1797-98, British Museum, London

Plate 43 of the book of etchings called *Los Caprichos* ("Follies") shows the artist asleep at his work desk surrounded by the creations of his imagination. The text that accompanies this print — possibly the best-known of the series — is translated as follows. "Imagination abandoned by reason produces impossible monsters: united with her she is the mother of the arts and the source of wonders."

FRANCISCO GOYA
The Forge
c 1812-15, Frick Collection, New York

Goya's originality was not merely a matter of technique: he also was one of the first artists to give a significant place in his work to the labouring classes. His depiction of these workers shows a deep understanding of the skilled co-ordination of movement such activity involves. This was one of the relatively few paintings by Goya to be seen in France — between 1838 and 1848 it was part of King Louis Philippe's "Spanish Gallery."

cratic beauty, the Duchess of Alba. A year later her husband died and Goya visited her residence at Sanlúcar de Barrameda, where he stayed for a number of months. He appears to have been deeply infatuated with her, although whether his feelings were reciprocated is unknown. Certainly she inspired some of his greatest works. After the death of his brother-in-law, Goya was appointed director of the Academy of Fine Arts, but his continuing ill-health forced him to resign from this position two years later. In the spring of 1798, he painted the frescoes of San Antonio de la Florida in Madrid, one of his great achievements.

The graphic works

In the autumn of 1799 Goya was given the supreme position of first court painter *(primer pintor de cámara del rey)*. The same year saw the publication of a suite of eighty-two etched and aquatinted plates entitled *Los Caprichos* ("Follies"), which firmly linked him with the liberal supporters of the Enlightenment. The etchings were based primarily on drawings he had made while staying with the Duchess of Alba at Sanlúcar, taken from

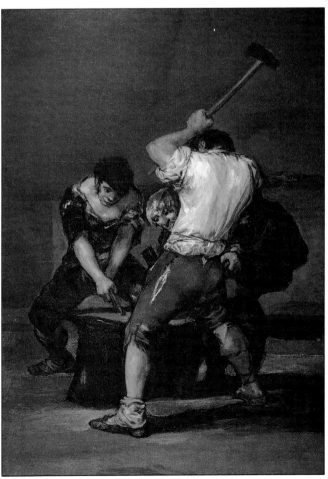

FRANCISCO GOYA
The Second of May 1808
1814, Prado, Madrid

The frenzy of killing is depicted with the frankness and vigour for which Goya is famous. This is not a propagandist glorification of war; it is a reaction to the horrific reality of violence and death. Goya takes no sides: the citizens fighting Murat's cavalry may be the heroes, but their savagery in the pursuit of their aims equals that of their oppressors.

scenes of everyday life at her residence, and revolving around the follies and superstitions of the Spanish people from every social sphere. He took enormous care with their production, and each plate is accompanied by a commentary and is given a succinct and evocative title that is at once comprehensible and disturbingly ambiguous. "No one knows himself," "There's plenty to suck," "And still they won't go," are just a few of the titles. As the introductory commentary makes clear, they represent "the follies and blunders common in every civil society as well as ... vulgar prejudices and lies authorized by custom, ignorance or interest ..." With startling economy of detail, Goya creates in these prints a murky urban wasteland fired with a theatrical tension and populated by a host of diverse individuals. It is at once specific and general, and the biting edge of his satire cuts many ways — even some of the institutions he attacked in the etchings praised the series as an edifying force. If Goya is to be believed, they were on sale for a mere two days and then withdrawn, possibly as a result of the intervention of the Inquisition. In 1803 Goya presented the king with the copper plates of *Los Caprichos* and 240 unsold copies of the printed book, receiving by way of compensation an annual pension of 12,000 reals for his son, Francisco Javier. The episode appears to have done him little harm. His Velasquez-inspired portrait of *Charles IV and his Family,* painted in 1800 (see page 37), ushered in a period of relative tranquility and wellbeing.

Political conflicts

On 17 March 1808, Ferdinand, Prince of the Asturias, heir to the Spanish throne, staged a *coup d'état* against his father Charles IV, whose reign had been repressive and consisted of an unparalleled series of disasters. The king and his corrupt minister Godoy were imprisoned, and on 19 March Charles abdicated in favour of his son, who became Ferdinand VII. Napoleon ordered the troops he had in Spain under a treaty made a year earlier, to occupy Madrid and six days later the French general Murat entered the city unopposed. On 2 May, the populace reacted to the occupation by attacking a detachment of mamelukes and dragoons escorting Charles IV's brother in one of the city's main squares, the Puerta del Sol. Reprisal was merciless and swift: forty-three civilians were executed on the hill of Principe Pio just outside the city. Goya witnessed these events, which gave rise to two major canvases (see page 55), painted after the final defeat of the French, when Spanish artists were given the opportunity to commemorate the uprising. Goya's versions were not popular with the government and were hidden away from public view for many years.

When Napoleon installed his brother Joseph Bonaparte on the throne (13 May), the anti-French revolt spread all over Spain. The Spanish royal family, held at the French town of Bayonne, sanctioned the *guerrilleros* — the first guerilla war had begun. It was this brutal and bloody conflict that Goya recorded in his powerful series of etchings, *The Disasters of War,* produced, ironically, at the same time as accepting the appointment of court painter to King Joseph.

The Duke of Wellington's forces slowly pushed the French out of Spain, and in 1814 Joseph abdicated. Ferdinand VII returned to the throne. He wasted no time in continuing the absolutist regime of his father, reinstituting the monastic orders and even restoring the Inquisition. From 1814 to 1820 some 12,000 Spaniards found guilty of French sympathies were arrested or sent into exile. Goya himself was tried for treason, but acquitted on a technicality.

It was a prolonged period of confusion, resulting in divided loyalties amongst liberals who, like Goya, had initially viewed France as the harbinger of reform. Goya's work records the travails of the time. The figure of the Colossus (see page 45) dominates his late painting and graphic work, much of which was meant as a private reacion to the futile horrors of war and its effects upon a civilian population. His views are ones we understand and are only too familiar with — there are few heroes, only victims. As a well-known former liberal and French sympathizer he was in real danger of persecution, and his prints connected with these years were not published until after his death.

Last years

Goya retired to the country, to a comfortable house on the banks of the river Manzanares near Madrid. His wife had died (in 1812), as had four of his five children. In 1819, aged seventy-three, he fell seriously ill but recovered and despite his age, began to experiment with the newly discovered medium of lithography, of which he is one of the most celebrated masters. He went on to produce some of his greatest works, those known as the "Black Paintings," executed directly onto the walls of his house. There are fourteen of these (now in the Prado), and with a certain sardonic humour, he placed the paintings of *Saturn Eating His Children* (inspired by an oil by Rubens of the same subject) and *Two Old People Eating* (see page 59) in his dining room. These magnificent and pessimistic productions were produced simultaneously with the equally enigmatic suite of etchings called the *Disparates* ("Absurdities"), reminiscent of the earlier *Caprichos.*

Goya had by now become a wealthy man, possessing substantial amounts of jewellery and property, and owning a collection of paintings by Rembrandt, Tiepolo, Velasquez and Correggio as well as seventy-three of his own works. However, although his relationship with the despotic monarch appears to have been relatively stable, the outlook was not promising, and Goya wasted no time

"There is no Remedy"
1810-11, British Museum,
London

This etching from Goya's *Disasters of War* series is a reduction to essentials of his painting *The Third of May* (see page 55). Three stakes, like three crucifixes, stand out starkly from the darkness, the victims anonymous, their dead bodies supported only by the ropes that bind them. Like so many of Goya's images, these cross the boundaries of time and place to speak to us today as clearly as when they were first drawn.

He continued to experiment with techniques and media, painting miniatures on ivory, and in 1823 producing the lithographs known as *Bulls of Bordeaux*. He seems to have been happy and content — certainly pictures like the *Milkmaid* suggest a certain ease with his lot. In May, 1826, he returned to Spain, where he was well received by the court, but he stayed only long enough to ensure that his pension was secure and then returned to Bordeaux. He died on 16 April, 1828, aged eighty-two, and was buried in France, fittingly, since it was there that his art was to make such an impact on both the avant-garde and the establishment painters of the 19th century. His body was not brought back to the country of his birth until 1901, when it was placed quite equally fittingly in the small church of San Antonio del Florida, which thirty years earlier he had decorated with images showing the full scope of his genius.

Still Learning
1824-28, Prado, Madrid

Goya continued to paint and draw, experimenting tirelessly with new media, until he died. This drawing, done when he was an eighty-year-old exile in France, is not an actual self-portrait, but is surely a metaphorical one. Like the works of other aged masters, such as Titian and Rembrandt, it is a testament to the unquenchable curiosity and creative inventiveness of its executor.

arranging his exit from Spain. He requested leave, "to take the waters of Plombières" (in France), but he made no attempt to reach the spa town and settled instead in Bordeaux. "Goya has come," wrote his friend and fellow exile Moratin, "deaf, old, slow and weak . . . but content and anxious to see the world." From June to the end of August 1824 he lodged in Paris, where he had a chance to see at the Salon the *Massacre of Chios* by the young Romantic painter, Eugène Delacroix — it is said that he was unimpressed. He returned to Bordeaux, and Moratin recorded that "Goya is full of himself and painting all that occurs to him, without ever spending time in correcting what he has already painted."

The Milkmaid of Bordeaux
c 1827, Prado, Madrid

This calm and assured portrait of a working girl was painted for the artist's own pleasure when he was living in France. He died a year after its completion. The young girl's shawl and blue-green dress palpitate with broken touches of colour, the warm red ground breaks through periodically to add a warmth to the cool tones that serve as the basis of the composition.

GOYA'S PAINTING METHODS

A Walk in Andalusia was painted, like many of Goya's works, on a warm reddish ground, which is allowed to show through to stand as the shadow area of the tunic.

Goya's frescoes, such as a *Miracle of St Anthony*, were squarely in the tradition of Baroque painting. Each figure is formed with a few telling strokes to create a simple but powerful effect.

The Black Paintings show Goya's virtuoso brushwork at its most personal, with the details slashed on with thick impasto over a dark ground.

Goya was one of the great manipulators of paint, like Titian, Rubens and Rembrandt. But the freedom of his technique, which made such an impact on 19th-century painters, was a direct continuation of the Baroque tradition, in which the fewest number of brushstrokes are exploited for maximum potential.

In Goya's time the traditional technique of building up the density of tones and colours by working in successive layers over a monochrome underpainting was still the norm, and it is the method he would have learned in his apprentice years. But later, notably when he became so successful as a portrait painter that he had to work extremely rapidly, he perfected the method of direct (or *alla prima*) painting that most artists now use — paint is premixed on the palette so that each brushstroke is an approximation to the finished tone and colour. Goya sometimes employed both methods in one work, using layers of delicate glazes in one part and painting wet into wet in others. He varied the colours of his grounds, sometimes using a dark priming and sometimes allowing the warm colour of a red priming to break through as a counterpoint to greys and cool colours. As he grew older his brushwork became more and more personal — we see dots, squiggles, lozenges, circles, narrow lines and thick ones, and he would apply paint with anything that was available, including his fingers.

Goya's output was prodigious, and he worked very fast, often completing a painting in no more than an hour. He rarely made use of background detail, and tended to limit his colour harmonies to two, or a clash of two main colours reconciled by harmonies. He particularly loved cool blue-greys and salmon pinks, and often used thinned black paint to establish details. In this self-portrait he has shown himself working with candles fixed around the band of his hat to provide a back-up light. This seems a somewhat bizarre device, but was evidently effective — it is recorded that he often finished his paintings by artificial light.

CHRONOLOGY OF GOYA'S LIFE

1746   30 March, Francisco José de Goya y Lucientes born at Fuendetodos.

1760   Begins four-year apprenticeship in the studio of José Luzán at Saragossa.

1763   Unsuccessful attempt to gain a scholarship to the Academy of San Fernando in Madrid.

1771   First commission: frescoes for the Pilar Cathedral at Saragossa.

1774   Invited by the Neo-classical artist, Raphael Mengs, to work for the Royal Tapestry works of Santa Barbara.

1775   First tapestry commissions.

1778   Begins a series of etchings after Velasquez's paintings.

1780   Successful reception of his painting *Christ on the Cross*. Unanimously elected a member of the Academy of San Fernando.

1784   Birth of his son Javier.

1785   Appointed assistant director of painting at the Academy of San Fernando.

1786   Appointed painter to the king.

1789   Coronation of Charles IV. Goya promoted to official court painter.

1791-2 Paints the last of his tapestry cartoons.

1792-3 Goya is stricken with a serious illness that leaves him profoundly deaf.

1795   Succeeds Francisco Bayeu as director of painting at the Academy of San Fernando.

1796   Stays with the recently widowed Duchess of Alba at her Sanlúcar estate.

1797   Announcement of the publication of *Los Caprichos*.

1798   Paints frescoes for the Church of San Antonio de la Florida, Madrid.

Don Manuel Osorio de Zuñiga

Doña Isabel Cobos de Porcel

The Burial of the Sardine

1799   Publication of *Los Caprichos*. Appointed first court painter.

1808   Napoleon's troops enter Spain, Joseph Bonaparte made king. Uprising in Madrid on 2 May and subsequent executions on 3 May.

1810   Works on the *The Disasters of War* etchings.

1811   Awarded the Royal Order of Spain by Joseph.

1814   Restoration of Ferdinand VII to the Spanish throne

1816   Publication of the *Tauromachia* series.

1819   Purchases House of the Deaf Man. Falls ill at the end of the year. Recovers to make first experiments with lithography.

1800   Paints *Charles IV and his Family*.

1804-5 Probable date of *Portrait of Dona Isabel Cobos de Porcel*.

1812-9 Paints *The Burial of the Sardine*.

1814   Paints two canvases commemorating uprising of 1808: *The Second of May* and *The Third of May*.

1820-2 Paints Black Paintings on wall of house.

1824   Goya goes into hiding as liberals suffer persecution. On 30 May he is allowed to leave Spain. Stays in Paris and then (September) settles in Bordeaux with a young German widow, Leocadia Weiss.

1825   Set of lithographs: *The Bulls of Bordeaux*. Paints a number of ivory miniatures.

1826   Brief sojourn in Madrid to secure pension. The painter Vincent Lopez paints his portrait.

1827   Second visit to Madrid since self-imposed exile.

1828   Dies on 16 April.

THE PAINTINGS

A Walk in Andalusia: Majas and the Muffled Majos

(tapestry cartoon)
August 1777
$108\frac{1}{4} \times 74\frac{3}{4}$in/$2.75 \times 1.9$m
Oil on canvas
Prado, Madrid

The gestures and poses of the figures betray the theatrical origins of this scene, in which the mood is at once decorative and melodramatic. The setting, in spite of the title, is not Andalusia but one of the many parks of Madrid. Like the work of the 18th-century French artist Antoine Watteau, the painting was designed to appeal to the cultivated tastes of the aristocracy, and the tapestry woven from it was destined for the dining room of the princes of the Asturias in the Prado Palace. The tones, colours and forms are all clearly demarcated to help the weavers transform the work into a successful textile design, but in later cartoons Goya became progressively less constrained by these limitations.

The colourful characters inhabiting Goya's designs are often, as in this case, taken from the demi-monde of the *majas* and *majos,* whose flamboyant dress and behaviour were often imitated by the upper and middle classes. They bore themselves with a haughty grandeur, the men wearing tight knee-breeches and stockings, ostentatiously buckled shoes, short jackets and a colourful *bandilero* around their waists in which lay hidden a *navaje,* or folding knife. The outfit was completed by the dark, dramatic swathes of a heavy black cloak and a low-brimmed hat. The women affected the same short jackets, and were potentially as dangerous as their partners, since a sharp dagger lay concealed beneath their wide skirts. The fiery romances of these people were popularized by the works of such dramatists as Roman de la Cruz, and by the time this painting was completed *majaism* had become a popular trend with the fashionable upper and middle classes.

In his paintings for the Santa Barbara tapestry works Goya's training in the Baroque tradition can clearly be seen. Effects are gained with the minimum of means and an apparent ease combined with an absolute mastery of technique. These canvases do not normally possess a particularly pronounced weave although the grain of the material is distinctly noticeable in the more thinly painted areas of the cartoon. The canvas was coated with a thin glue size, and on top of this was placed a coat of coloured tempera. Over this ground a coat of fairly thick oil paint was brushed to create a comparatively smooth base for the painting.

The colour of Goya's ground is easily discernible and was always employed to give a warmth to the overall composition and to enhance the decorative effect of the image. Whenever he could take a short cut by using this warm ground as a positive element in his picture he did so. An example of this can be seen in the bodice of the *maja,* in which Goya has only applied the blue paint to denote the colour of the velvet material, allowing the red ground to work most effectively as the shadowy area of her tunic. This practice allowed the overall colouration of the composition to remain light and airy. Goya used a red clay colour for these initial stages — Seville earth which, when mixed with white, resulted in a brick-red tone that could be either left as a colour in its own right or modified by the glazes that he used so inventively. In later works he lightened the tone of this base colour to a cool pinkish hue.

Goya was only one of a number of artists who produced works specifically designed to be translated into tapestries by the skilled workers of the Santa Barbara tapestry factory. Although the production of these cartoons was something of a chore for the artist, his work in this field gave him a valuable grounding in technique and composition, which he turned to account in much of his later, more personal work.

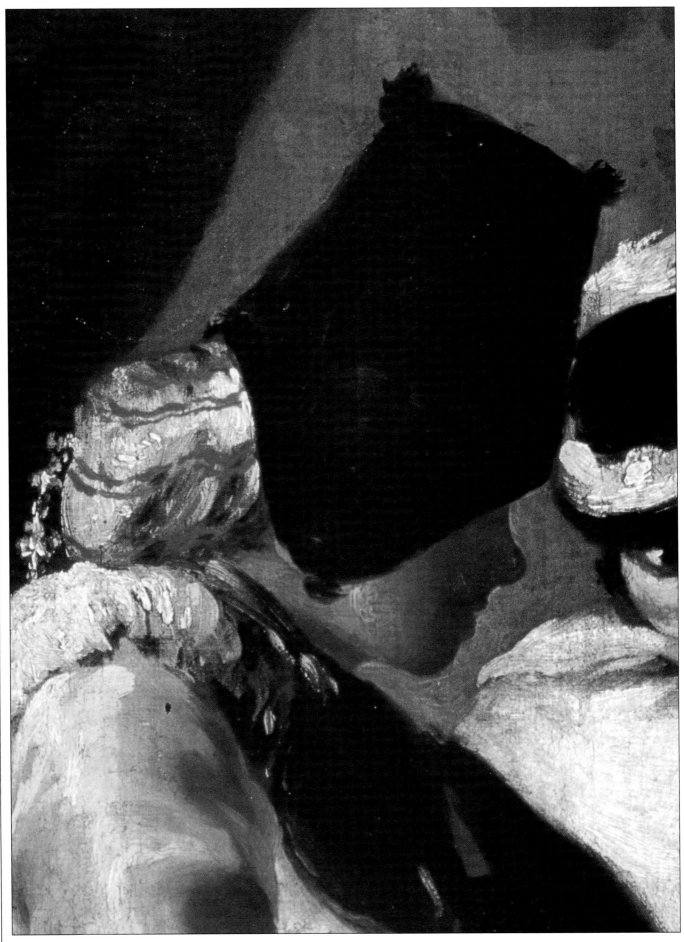

1 *Actual size detail*

2

1 *Actual size detail* Goya's inventive mark making, use of impasto and innovative freedom in use of colour can be clearly seen in this detail, particularly in the *majo's* distinctive bandeau where the variously handled layers of pigment work together to create, at the right visual distance, a stunning sense of actuality.

2 Goya frequently painted on a pink ground, which allowed greater speed of execution. The way he uses the colour within the composition constantly changes. Sometimes it helps to define objects, while elsewhere it is used to enhance the decorative qualities of the colours laid over it. Here it signifies not only the shadows in the heavily worked brocade, but also the more supple areas of the sleeve. Deft loops of paint added to the impastoed yellow combine to give a sumptuous and suitably gaudy richness.

3 In this area of the painting the pink ground colour is clearly visible between the brushstrokes that define the material. So skilfully does Goya manipulate the presence of the ground colour that it is sometimes difficult to ascertain where the underpainting is allowed to show. Separate slashes of green, blue, black and white create the dazzling illusion of the sash.

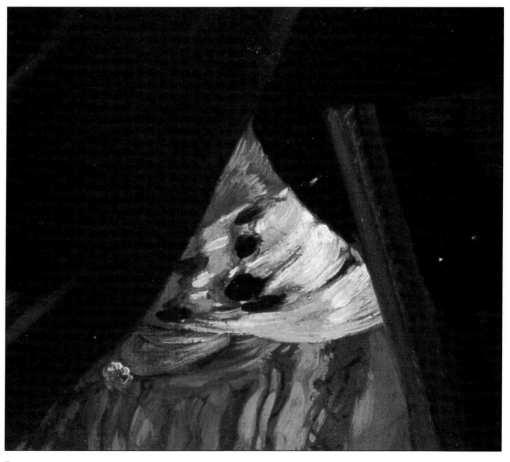

3

DON MANUEL OSORIO DE ZUÑIGA

c 1788-9

50×39³/₄in/127×101cm

Oil on canvas

Metropolitan Museum of Art, New York

The subject of this arresting canvas is Manuel Osorio Manrique de Zuñiga, the four-year-old son of the Count de Altimira. Isolated and vulnerable, his doll-like stance and expressionless features create a powerful aura of fragile innocence. The painting is an icon of aristocratic power: the young child waits, ready for the burdens of responsibility and position that his parents expect of him. There is something deeply poignant about this painting. The magpie, held prisoner by a thin piece of string, is protected from the rapacious cats that gaze so greedily at it by the presence of this geisha-like mannequin. A further commentary on power, captivity and control is suggested not only by the birds in the cage, but by the painter's own card, which is held lightly in the beak of the captive bird. As the cats watch the bird so this young boy is watched by those who control his destiny.

This bitter-sweet painting relies heavily upon the works of Velasquez and the British portraitists of the 18th century, who were imitated throughout Europe. Goya may not have known any original works by Gainsborough or Reynolds, but he would have had access to engravings of their paintings. The child's large dark chestnut coloured eyes complement his brown hair which, in the manner of Velasquez, is lightly stroked with touches of sepia. The brushstrokes are laid close together, with the artist's bravura painting style given free rein only in the painting of the white satin sash. The most striking element of the composition is the startling mass of scarlet that describes the boy's suit so simply and completely. It is barely modulated, and yet despite the sharpness of the silhouette against the background, a palpable impression of his clothing is given by the way Goya has artfully broken up the block of colour with carefully placed white accents of satin and lace.

The boy is set against a cool yellowish grey which is modulated by the fall of light. There are two conflicting sources of light. The facial features are lit from behind the viewer, a technique often found in the paintings of Edouard Manet later in the 19th century. The background play of light and dark falling in a diagonal from the top left-hand side of the canvas highlights the area immediately behind the boy's head and causes a band of light to reach up from the lower left to illuminate the magpie, Goya's card, the boy's feet and the caged birds — significantly the cats are left in shadow. The lighting of the portrait is purely artistic, as is the imagined space within which the boy is placed. A vertical to the right of the canvas is suggestive of a depth that is contradicted by the disposition of the trio of cats to the right.

The inscription on the card held in the magpie's beak bears the artist's signature: Dn Franco Goya.

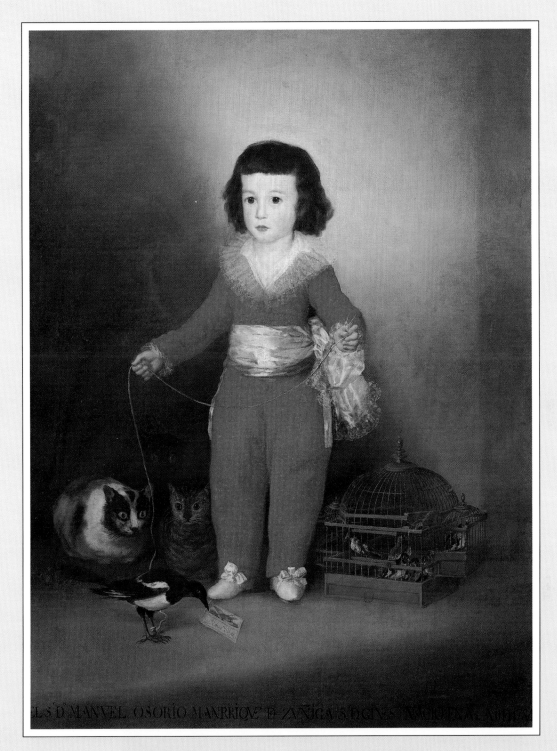

This portrait belongs to the first year of Goya's dominance in portrait painting. From this year until the Peninsular War he was the principal portraitist in Spain, and was inundated with commissions. His portraits differ markedly from those of his contemporaries, whose paintings often seem lifeless and stiff in comparison with works such as this. Despite the sitter's doll-like appearance, there is a powerful impression of a living being. The artist's unconventional handling of space which causes the foreground to drop away from the viewer creates a strong visual bond between us and the painted image.

1

2

1 The techniques seen in this detail of Don Manuel's hand bear close similarities with those of Velasquez, whose work Goya had closely studied. The modelling is as restrained and underplayed as it is in the work of the earlier master, and equally similar is Goya's use of red to give the effect of the warmth and firmness of human flesh. The translucent delicacy of the boy's lace cuff is suggested by the same skilful and inventive use of the key colour.

2 The placing of the artist's card in the captive bird's beak is at once a sharp-edged comment about his perception of the artist/patron relationship and a simple and novel way of introducing his signature into the painting.

3 *Actual size detail* This small but significant accent of red, repeated between the open brushwork indicating the sash, helps suggest a roundness of form to what would otherwise be a very flat silhouette of almost unmodulated red. Such accents, which Goya had assimilated from his study of the works of Velasquez, can be seen used to equal effect in Edouard Manet's *Fife Player* of 1866. Goya's son mentions that his father often worked by candle-light, particularly when he was applying the finishing touches to his canvases. It is possible that the quality of light in this painting owes something to this practice.

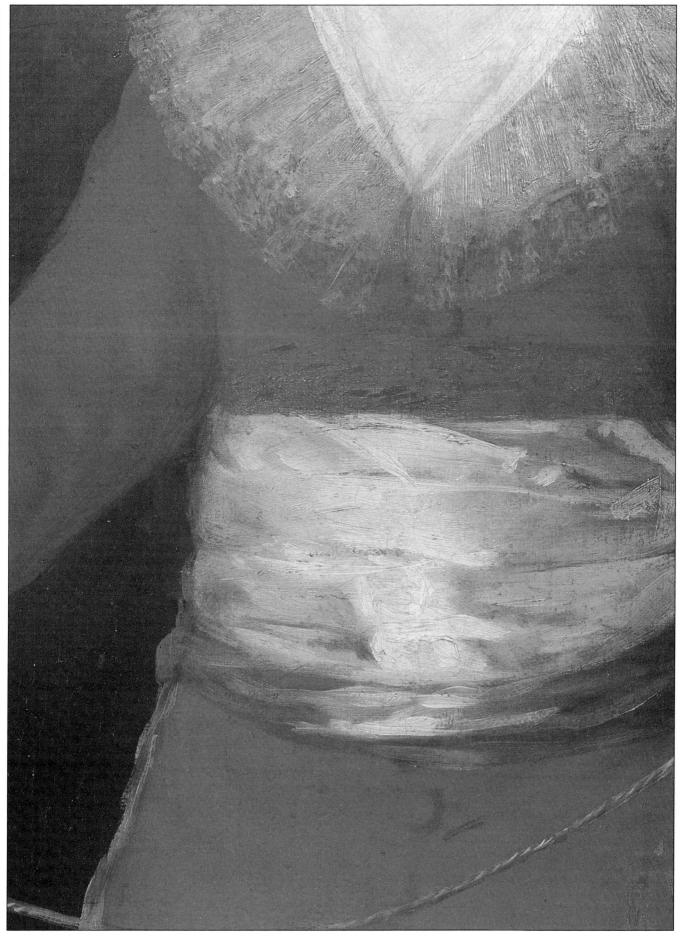

3 *Actual size detail*

THE BEWITCHED: PRIEST POURING OIL ON THE DEVIL'S LAMP

1797-98
16½×11¾in/42×30cm
Oil on canvas
National Gallery, London

This was one of six small witchcraft scenes commissioned by the Duke and Duchess of Osuna, for which the artist was paid 6000 reales, a considerable amount of money at the time. The Osuna family were among Goya's earliest and most supportive patrons. The duchess was a great lover of the arts, the theatre and the bullfight, and it is likely that this series of paintings reflected her interests rather than those of the duke. In 1799 Goya sold to her no less than four sets of *Los Caprichos,* which consisted of eighty prints in the first edition. The paintings were produced at the same time that he was working on these etchings, and they and the paintings correspond in both subject and composition. Such scenes were highly fashionable in the liberal intellectual circles in which Goya and the Osunas moved. Eleven years earlier the Osunas had commissioned him to produce a large oil painting for the family chapel in the Cathedral of Valencia depicting St Francisco de Borja, an ancestor of the duchess, at the death-bed of a penitent. In this work, his earliest known depiction of the supernatural, blood flows miraculously from the crucifix proffered by the saint to save the dying man from the ghouls that surround his bed.

In its simple divisions of tone and its use of a single sombrely dressed figure, *The Bewitched* could be read as a parody on Velasquez's masterful paintings of philosophers that Goya had copied earlier in his career. The painting relates directly to a popular play written in the late 17th century by Antonio de Zamora. The book visible in the right-hand corner of the painting bears the inscription LAM DESCO, which is a reference to a speech in the play which begins "*Lámpara descomunal* [monstrous lamp] . . ."

The bewitched priest has the illusion that his life will only continue as long as the lamp in the painting remains lit. Quite sensibly, therefore, if with an understandable degree of fear, he pours oil to feed the flame. The brilliant colour of the flame creates a dramatic contrast with the monochromatic treatment of the rest of the canvas, while the spotlight effect on the priest's almost caricatured features reveals the intensity of his terror. A horizontal dash of light draws attention to his feet, which are humourously juxtaposed with the cloven hooves of the hermaphrodite devil who holds out the lamp with mock servility. Behind the two figures, a group of donkeys rear out from the shadows to witness this strange scene. The light, almost farcical humour seen in the painting is absent from the gritty nightmare world of *Los Caprichos.*

Goya's concern with the supernatural remained a constant in his art. At the end of his life he returned to such subjects in his Black Paintings, in which, stripped of their anecdotal qualities, they reappear as some of the most powerful meditations on the human condition in Western art.

The humour of this small cabinet painting can still be appreciated today, but the obvious anecdotal quality of the work should not be allowed to obscure our appreciation of its painterly qualities. The construction is tightly knit, resting upon the meticulously balanced gradations of light and dark. The fresh and lively handling of the paint surface further unites the separate elements of the composition to create a pleasing decorative ensemble.

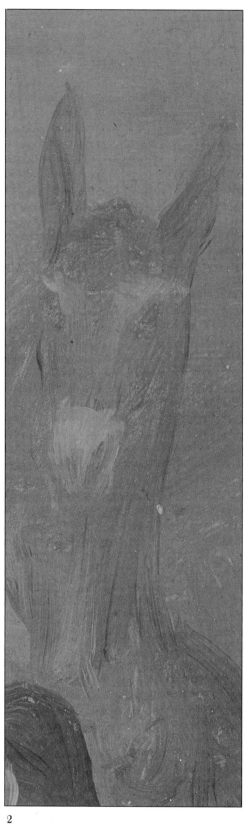

1

2

1 The devil's head emerges out of the darkness, indicated only by those parts of its anatomy which catch the rather unconvincingly powerful light emanating from the lamp.

2 The ghostly images of the rearing donkeys are lightly sketched in a few tones. The warm colour of the ground and the grey of the underpainting allow the creatures to form a dominant part of the background while at the same time giving the impression of melting into it.

3 A variety of Goya's techniques can be clearly seen in these details. Goya moves from the merest of indications to a more detailed working, as is evident in the handling of the priest's face, the dramatic centre of this small painting. Carefully drawn details such as the raised hand suggest a sense of finish that is absent from the rest of the picture. The warm ground Goya liked to use can be clearly sensed in all parts of the painting, giving a richness and glow to the predominantly cool tones.

3

A Miracle of St Anthony

1798

(detail)

Fresco

San Antonio de la Florida

Goya and his assistant Asensi Juliá painted the cupola and supporting decorations of the hermitage of San Antonio de la Florida in 1798. In reverse of traditional practice, a heavenly throng of angels supports the all too-human world that makes up the subject matter of the painting. The story is relatively simple. St Anthony's father had been accused of murder, and in order to prove his innocence the saint was prevailed upon to resuscitate the corpse of the murdered man. The fresco shows the very moment of the miracle, with St Anthony surrounded by about fifty figures of both sexes and various ages and social position. Each shows a different degree of interest in the unusual event. Some raise their hands and faces in ecstasy, while others, less easily impressed or perhaps unaware of the miraculous nature of the resuscitation, indulge in the more normal activities of a crowd. To the left of the saint, balancing the form of an old man in yellow who might be his father, is a man in a yellow jerkin and slouch hat who turns to force his way through the crowd — the murderer perhaps?

The first impression on entering the chapel is one of clarity and light. The centre of the dome is topped by a lantern whose pierced sides form both the actual source of light and the imaginary illumination for the composition. In accordance with the architecture of the church, the colouration of the fresco is based around greys — almost unbelievable in their range — counterpointed by broad swathes of low-toned colour. The varied tones of grey are activated by the presence throughout the fresco of black and white and by separate groups of various single colours that are placed in a rhythmical order across the composition. The painted balustrade continues the line of the architecture, and creates a vivid sense of space and actuality. The crowd leans, climbs or falls away from this railing, while swathes of material, human limbs or the falling folds of sleeves break up its stark geometry. The overwhelming sensation is one of movement and human drama. Once again Goya's training in the Baroque tradition and his experience as a tapestry designer has allowed him to work with an astonishing abbreviation of technique and a sureness of touch that places him firmly in the company of the 17th-century Italian painters, such as Luca Giordiano and Tiepolo. These great decorative painters were among many who had found employment in Spain, carrying out grand fresco schemes for the royal palaces.

Goya's technique was that of *buon fresco*, painting directly onto the still wet plaster in a free and spontaneous way, and forming the figures with a few expressive slashes of his brush. In each figure there are two or three major shifts of tone; Goya's tonal accuracy allowed him to situate his figures in the imagined space of the dome using the minimal amount of detail, making the entire work, when seen from below, throb with the pulse of real life. The cupola is relatively small, and although the figures are over life-size, the general effect is one of intimacy, with each figure clearly identifiable. Not least of Goya's achievements was that the fresco took him less than three months to complete.

In the Baroque tradition, the painting aims at creating a clear and powerful effect — such works were not produced to be seen as masterpieces of painting, but as dramatic narratives. The modern viewer, taking a close-up view with binoculars or telephoto lenses, can discern parallels with 19th- and 20th-century Expressionism, but for Goya such effects were simply the result of the methods employed to overcome technical problems. Nor were they unique to Goya, as is shown by a treatise on Spanish painting by Palomino written in the early 18th century.

Goya produced a number of paintings for churches in his early career, and this is one of the finest examples in the whole of 18th-century church decoration. Goya, who had petitioned the king for the commission (San Antonio was owned by the crown), was in total artistic control of the project. Following customary practice, he claimed for enough painting materials to last him a number of years after the completion of the work. The small church, which now contains the artist's tomb, is one of his most secure claims to fame.

1

1 Fresco painting demands an absolute sureness of technique because few alterations can be made. Goya completed this commission within 120 days. It was painted *al fresco*, the pigments being dissolved in limewater and painted directly onto specially prepared wet plaster. This, as it dries, becomes part of the physical structure of the wall, with any underdrawing (or *sinopia*) obliterated in the process. Once dry, a few additional touches can be laid across the surface to further define the image. These details show that Goya treated all the various elements of his composition as painterly problems to be solved in the most direct and simple way possible. Such thinking allowed him to make the most extraordinary and effective "short-hand" notations for the people and other elements that fill his composition.

2 The dramatic rhythms of Goya's staccato brushstrokes have the vigour and force of a modern expressionistic painter, and his freedom in this recalcitrant medium equals that seen in his oil paintings. An interplay of simple masses and constructional marks creates a totally convincing image of these three women lost in reverie.

3 The most complicated of effects are translated into the simplest of technical operations involving an ever-changing use of over-painting with opaque or translucent paint.

2

3

1

1 The limited colour range of the fresco can be well appreciated in this detail. The basic blue-grey balance is counterpointed by dramatic touches of the primary colours. Goya's task was to paint a fresco that had to be read from a distance, hence his exaggerations and simple dramatic shifts of tone and colour. These, when seen from the floor of the church, are vivid and convincing, retaining the vitality of actual life.

2 The spectators each make their own reaction to the miracle taking place in their presence. This young boy's expression of awe and repulsion is brilliantly caught in a few deft brushstrokes. His upturned face is placed in space by the directional broken touches evident in the fair hair and in the single mark that defines his chin. The white overpainting of the sleeve and ragged leggings contrast with broad sweeps that indicate the larger masses of the painting, contrasts that add to the sense of vitality that permeates the composition.

3 Three simple areas of paint create the illusion of a fully rounded human being. Directional brushstrokes describe the anatomical structures of the figures with brilliant economy of means. The features are fixed with an equal freedom of technique, a few judicious white highlights scumbled across the surface with a dry brush bringing the whole into relief.

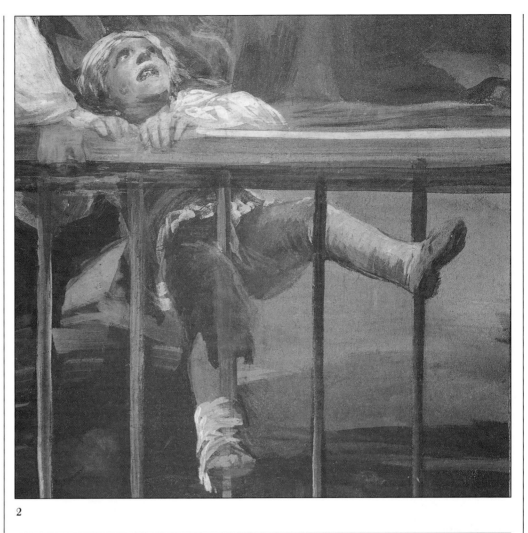

2

3

CHARLES IV AND HIS FAMILY

1800
100×132½in/254×336.5cm
Oil on canvas
Prado, Madrid

In an age like our own that tends to associate glamour with power, the apparent honesty of Goya's treatment of these obviously less than perfect human beings may come as something of a shock. There are few other royal portraits that can match the brutal frankness of this depiction of the realities of hereditary monarchy. And yet the royal family were apparently pleased with the painting; Queen Maria Luisa wrote of the sketches (which are even less flattering than the final version), "Tomorrow Goya is beginning another portrait of me. He has finished the others [for the family group] and they are all very well done." Nearly half a century later, the 19th-century French poet and critic Théophile Gautier described the king and his family as looking like "the corner baker and his wife after they have won the lottery."

The work has obvious parallels with Velasquez's famous *Las Meninas* (see page 7), which is, amongst other things, an informal portrait of the Infanta and her royal parents. Goya had copied the painting as a learning exercise earlier in his career, and the reference to the Velasquez family group would have been appreciated by the royal family, as it linked them through the painting to the illustrious "Golden Age" of Spanish history.

On 22 April, 1800, the artist was summoned to the summer palace in order to paint the entire royal family, and less than two months later, on 13 June, the work was finished. It is very much a studio concoction, produced from a number of rapidly painted portrait sketches. The standing figure in blue is the king's eldest son, Ferdinand, who was later to lead a successful *coup d'état* against his father (see page 12). The girl who stands next to him, her face turned to the wall, could perhaps signify his as yet unidentified future bride. At the centre of the painting is the real controller of Spain's destiny, the matriarchal figure of the Bourbon queen, flanked by her youngest children. To her left is her husband — king in name, but overshadowed, both in the painting and in real life, by the more dominant personality of his wife. The nature of the composition and the brilliant characterization of the individual personages ensure that the eye of the viewer returns again and again to the secondary members of the group. The eyes of the majority of the family are focused with varying degrees of intensity out from the canvas at the viewer, who now occupies the position originally taken by the artist. Part of the painting's chilling atmosphere comes from the way Goya has placed himself in a position which would in reality be impossible. We can see the corner of his canvas on the extreme left of the painting, while he stands facing us, half-hidden in the shadows, shrewdly surveying the motley group of humanity it is his job to immortalize.

Even today, nearly 200 years after Goya "fixed" the Spanish royal family on canvas, the imperious stare of Queen Maria Luisa has enough regal power to stop casual strollers through the Prado in their tracks. Paintings such as these were the means by which royal authority could be disseminated via prints to a broader audience, and most were flattering portrayals. Goya, however, painted what he saw, and it is still a matter of some amazement that this disquietingly frank image of the Spanish Bourbon household was accepted by its sitters.

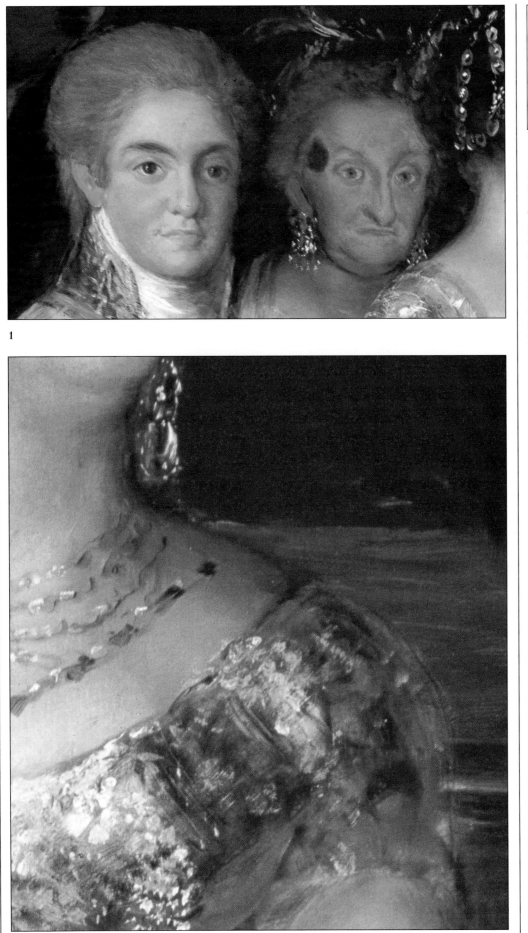

1

1 Certainly Goya's most flattering portrayal of the Prince of the Asturias, Ferdinand, monarch-to-be. The woman to his left is Doña Maria Josefa, the elder sister of the king, who died shortly after the painting was finished. Both figures, set in Hogarthian contrast to each other, are vivid examples of Goya's apparently objective stance and extraordinary powers of character analysis.

2 Goya's varied brushwork allows him to contrast the cosmeticized smoothness of the queen's flesh against the rich fabric of her dress. A few scribbles of dilute paint suggest her necklace and define her form, whilst a broken ribbon of rectangular marks of blue pigment are all that is needed to create the impression of glittering sapphires. Thickly impasted paint laid over the modulated browns of the background paint brings out the glitter of the earring.

3 *Actual size detail* The flashy gaudiness of Charles IV's decorations are perfectly matched by the explosive power of Goya's handling. Detail is sacrificed for effect, the sharp brightness of the medals described entirely by the surfaces that reflect the light. The thickly painted decorations are laid over thinly applied paint modulated by the warm ground colour beneath, and this area is in turn surrounded by more solidly applied brown paint that describes the rest of the king's coat.

2

3 *Actual size detail*

Doña Isabel Cobos de Porcel

1804-5/6?
32¼×21¼in/82×54cm
Oil on canvas
National Gallery, London

This is one of the most majestic of Goya's portraits. The magnificent aristocrat beauty is shown following the fashion of the time by dressing in the *maja* style, one associated with the inhabitants of the Madrid slums, but taken up by the rich and fashionable. The sitter, Doña Isabella Lobo y Mendieta, was the wife of Don Santonio de Porcel, a favourite of the all-powerful Manuel Godoy, the *éminence grise* of Spanish politics. The date of the painting is not absolutely certain, but it was probably the one that was exhibited at the San Fernando Academy in 1805; in 1806 Goya painted a companion portrait of her husband, which unfortunately no longer exists.

Many of Goya's portraits show acute psychological insights, but there is no place in this work for character analysis; the painting is concerned with the creation of an imposing image of confidence — in her sexuality and, most important, in her social position. This confidence is matched by the sumptuous brilliance with which the artist has constructed her image, one which sums up the spirit of the aristocratic class to which she belongs. Her figure fills the entire canvas, creating a marvellous glowing contrast of black and gold, enlivened by the artificial colour of her heavily made-up face. Goya's choice of a half-length format has allowed him to make the most of the dynamic possibilities of the costume, but apart from this, there are no auxiliary props to indicate her position or interests.

None is needed: the spiralling forms of her dark rose gown and her black mantilla rise up to support and frame her face and golden hair, and her form, melting into the neutral background, creates an image of strength and elegance.

Goya's son reported that "portrait painting came quite easily to him, and the most felicitous were those of his friends which he finished in a single sitting. He only worked for one session each day, sometimes ten hours at a stretch, but never in the afternoon. The last touches for the better effect of a picture he gave at night, by artificial light." The speed with which the artist worked has allowed the paint to form a single skin, the individual brushstrokes standing proud from each other in places, while in others they merge into each other to create a harmonious, unbroken paint surface.

The sitter's pose is rather unusual: the hands, half hidden by the sleeves of her *maja* jacket, suggest that she is either leaning on some kind of support or seated — it is difficult to decide which is the case. The tonality of the painting comes from the contrast between the warmth of the flesh tones and the rose pinks of her jacket and the magnificent black and green that dominates the rest of the canvas. The whites of the *fichu* are painted with heavy impasto, while the thin paint and light treatment of the black mantilla suggests the delicate, transparent quality of the lace, partially covering the rose satin jacket.

The almost overpowering presence of the aristocratic beauty, which almost threatens to spill out of its frame, disguises the fact that like so many of Goya's portraits it is very freely painted. Scribbles of paint overlay patches of colour, the thinnest of glazes are placed adjacent to thick, flat areas of buttery paint, which in this case match perfectly the cosmetics that the sitter has applied to her face. Goya's supreme technical assurance can be judged by the fact that this portrait was painted directly over an earlier one of a man, traces of which can still be discerned today (left).

1

2

3

1 X-ray and infra-red photography have been particularly helpful in studying the genesis and original state of Goya's paintings. Few can offer as spectacular a revelation as this example taken during a recent cleaning of the painting, and revealing the traces of a portrait of a man directly under the paint surface of the present work.

2 The thick paint denoting the broad areas of flesh on the sitter's face correspond to the cosmetics she wears, while more dilute paint is used to suggest the hollows and shadows. The handling gives a marvellous impression of the soft translucency of the sitter's skin, while her luxuriant coiffure is described with great economy.

3 The hand and sleeve are treated with wonderfully free, calligraphic brushstrokes, with a wide variety of subtle pinks, creamy yellows and warm greens used to build up the forms.

4 *Actual size detail* The unflagging inventiveness of Goya's handling was much admired by later painters in England and France. These have sometimes been referred to as "twist of the wrist" painters in acknowledgement of their attempts to match the athletic brushwork of Goya and Velasquez. The effect of the black lace has been created by streaking thin paint over the impasto of the white *fichu* and rose-pink jacket.

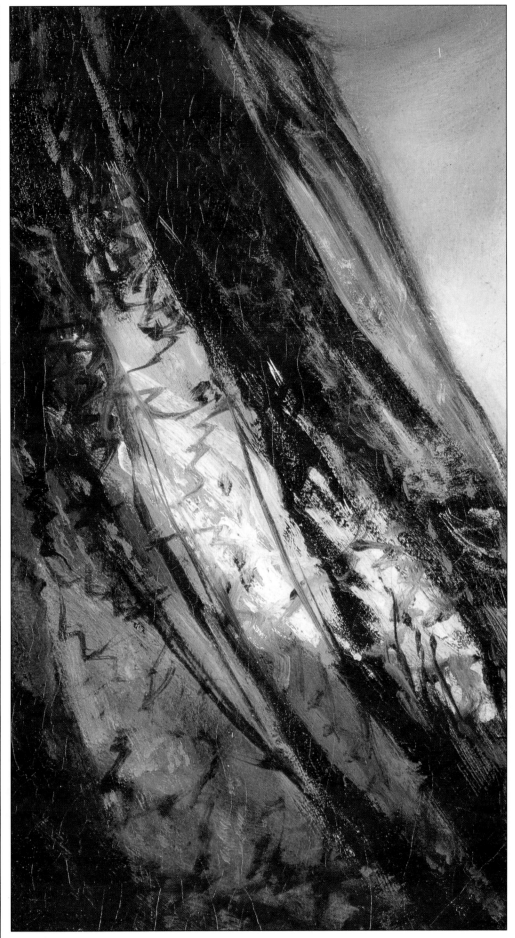

4 *Actual size detail*

THE COLOSSUS

(Goya's original title *The Giant*)
c 1809-12
$45^3/_8 \times 41^3/_8$ in/ 116×105 cm
Oil on canvas
Prado, Madrid

A huge naked figure strides blindly through an arid landscape, leaving panic and chaos in its wake. Without the giant, the painting becomes an image immediately familiar to us from any number of photographs of civil uprising and natural disaster. Goya has disregarded the artistic conventions for depicting such events, showing people and animals fleeing in all directions, while a single donkey stands immobile — an effective counterpoint to the dramatically lit mass of the giant and the surrounding mêlée. There is no explicit narrative to give a basis for interpretation of the picture: it could well be that the people are refugees already in flight from some other more mundane disaster across whose path has stumbled this fellow refugee from the world of dream or legend. It has been convincingly argued, however, that the immediate inspiration was a poem by Juan Bautista Arriza concerning the invasion of the French troops in 1808. This contains the following passage: *"On a height above yonder cavernous amphitheatre a pale colossus rises, caught by the fiery light of the setting sun; the Pyrenees are a humble plinth for his gigantic limbs."*

The painting has many of the conventions of a theatrical backdrop or tapestry design. The linear recession is summary — a simple system of locking diagonals which was common in Goya's work serves to suggest the landscape, whose scale and geological structure is completely at odds with the physical presence of the massive figure. But it is pre-cisely the conflicting relationship between these two elements that generates the hypnotic power of the picture. To accommodate the full figure of this Rodinesque giant the gentle undulations of the landscape would have to suddenly drop away several hundred feet beyond the horizon. For all the figure's convincing physicality, these illogical elements reinforce the spectral, as opposed to merely physical, reality of the apparition.

The painting was apparently one of those that the elderly artist produced for his own pleasure, and could easily be seen as part of the series of Black Paintings (see page 59). Careful examination of one of the latter group, *The Fight with Clubs*, reveals that the combatants are painted over a pre-existing landscape, the resulting incongruity of scale suggesting that they too could be of supernatural height.

The treatment of these later paintings is bold and free. Ceán Bermúdez, one of Goya's patrons, wrote that "I have seen my friend Don Francisco Goya paint with his fingers and with the point of a knife," while the artist's son noted two years after his father's death that Goya's "... own predilection was for the paintings he kept in his house, since he was free to paint them as he pleased. In this way he came to paint some of them with a palette knife instead of brushes." These, according to another of Goya's friends, Father Tomás López, were "little bamboo or cane knives [that] he made himself and was proud of inventing."

Goya's use of a high viewpoint has added to the impact of this powerful visionary painting. The landscape falls away from the viewer, creating a sense of vertigo that becomes increasingly acute as we appreciate the smallness of the figures and animals below compared with the huge bulk of the striding giant. The brute strength of the colossus is suggested not only by his aggressive pose, but also by his closed or downcast eyes — which might suggest, perhaps, that his rational mind is sleeping or non-existent, giving him the force of a natural phenomenon.

1

1 Goya worked in all media with an equal freedom and mastery of technique. In this work, painted for his own pleasure, he makes much use of the palette knife to create a richly textured paint surface. The effects are clearly visible in the cloud area reproduced here; the paint is applied thickly and spontaneously to match the free rolling forms through which the giant cleaves his monstrous way. The palette knife technique was not unknown at the time, and earlier painters, such as Rembrandt, had applied impasto with a knife in some areas of their paintings, but it was not used with an assurance to match Goya's until the French painters of the latter part of the 19th century took it up.

2 *Actual size detail* Separately applied dollops of pigment are set against each other to create the dramatically abbreviated impressions of people fleeing in panic, the idiosyncratic poses described by no more than one or two drawn lines. The small areas of colour contrast tellingly with the murky darks and ochres that make up the predominant colour harmonies of the painting.

2 *Actual size detail*

THE BURIAL OF THE SARDINE

c 1812-19
32½×24⅜in/82.5×62cm
Oil on panel
San Fernando Academy, Madrid

The date of this painting has been contested, but the period 1812-19 has now been generally accepted. It is a relatively small work, and depicts a procession that celebrates the Corpus Christi Festival on Ash Wednesday. The burial of a sardine, marking the end of Carnival time and the beginning of Lent, is a tradition that still continues in a modified form in the present day. In Goya's time, the celebrants would carry a puppet down to the bank of a river, where it was ceremonially burned. Like so many of his earlier tapestry designs, the work contains elements that were later to come to the fore in the Black Paintings (see page 59). Similar subjects had been painted by the Venetian artist, Giambattista Tiepolo, but Goya's knowledge of the work of the Northern European painters such as Hieronymus Bosch and Pieter Bruegel, who has treated similar themes in a more macabre way, stressing the inevitable triumph of death, has allowed him to instil this scene of bucolic entertainment with an all-pervasive atmosphere of terror.

Preliminary studies for the composition show that the banner originally bore the single word "Mortus" (death) in place of the huge grinning face that dominates the near-hysterical Carnival — "for remember dust thou art and to dust shalt thou return." In an attempt to arrest the inevitable progress of time, the celebrants dance in a frenzy; masks and disguises are worn and identities confused as individual responsibility is abdicated to the will of the crowd. *Picaros* and soldiers, animals and devils, mingle with those who look on, some of whom point out the more bizarre costumes, whilst others shudder in discomfiture at the unruly sight. From this swirling mass of movement the dancers are singled out by their white dresses. At first glance they appear to be radiantly happy, but closer examination proves this to be a false reading: the grins are not theirs but those of their masks, and one of their number — the figure on the right of the group — is, despite his dress, male. Shards of cool blue and blood red intermingle with a medley of ochres and greys. The brilliant patches of colour contrast with the mass of the banner and the swept-in areas of blue and green that nonchalantly indicate the landscape and sky — a little more than a painted backdrop. Goya's rapid, summary handling of the procession gives an impression of unrestrained movement: figures are caught in mid-action, some painted in sharp detail; others merely suggested by free and sketchy brushwork. The animation of the crowd is matched by the technical means Goya uses to describe it. Calligraphic traces of thin black paint interweave over commas, patches and blurs of pigment to create a balletic movement of brushstrokes across the canvas. Here we can see the roots of some of the startling innovations of Edouard Manet that were to have such consequences for French avant-garde art of the 19th century. Manet admitted a considerable debt to both Goya and Velasquez.

The world of 18th-century Spain was particular to itself, and one should be wary of creating over-simplistic comparisons with the present day. However, in this painting, as in many of Goya's works, we can recognize the sense of the ordinary world on the verge of slipping in the midst of celebration into something monstrous and terrible, where the rules that govern normal existence no longer apply. Goya's use of courtly or ecclesiastical ritual and masquerade are metaphors that an audience of today can still understand.

1 *Actual size detail*

1 *Actual size detail* By using thin black paint drawn over loosely laid-in areas of colour, Goya has created an impression of rich detail and enormous vitality. His calligraphic line weaves across the canvas defining and suggesting the heads and features of these grotesques. It is often difficult to decide whether Goya's creations are masked or otherwise, but what appears from a distance as a happy smile on the left-hand dancer's face is clearly the fixed grin of a mask. The dancer is quite possibly a man, despite the female costume.

2 This is one of the many ambiguous and possibly malevolent figures in the crowd whose identity and purpose defy definition. Goya has selected the degree of finish and detail in each area of the painting, thus creating a richness and sense of life that is analogous to real experience. As someone watching the event might search out a particular focus of interest, peripheral areas of activity would fade out of focus.

2

3

3 Goya exploits the colour of the ground to great effect in his works. Here his assurance is evident in his economical handling. He allows the medium to describe all that is essential about the figure — his dress, and his aggressive and ambiguous posturing — but never allows himself to be beguiled by unnecessary details that could weaken his statement.

4 The rhythmic flow of Goya's line as it weaves in and out of patches of colour has the effect of reinforcing the action it describes.

5 The drawing of this woman and child looking on is a good example of the way in which Goya can develop a sense of character and movement with great economy of means.

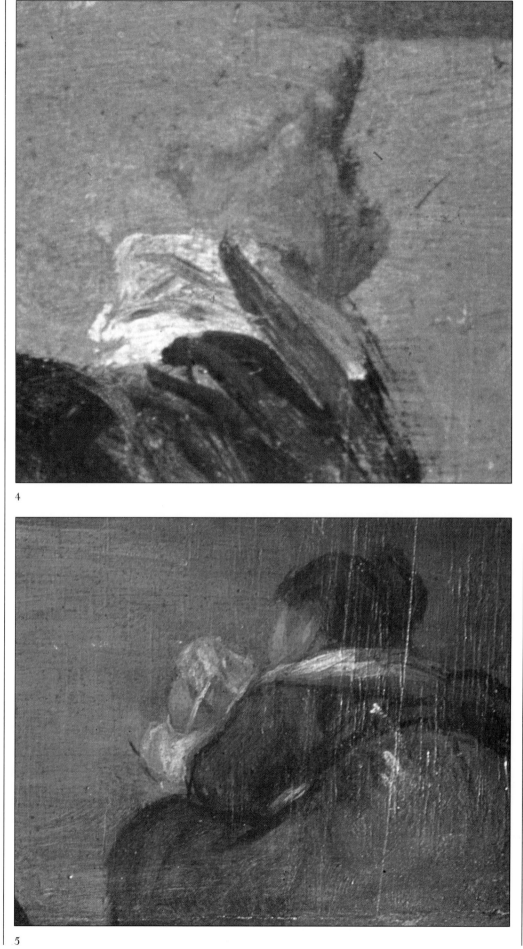

4

5

THE THIRD OF MAY 1808

1814

104½×136in/2.66×3.45m

Oil on canvas

Prado, Madrid

The two canvases which commemorate the Uprising of 2 May 1808 were painted six years after the events took place. 2 May was the day on which the *canaille* of Madrid reacted to the French occupation by attacking General Murat's cavalry. The next morning terrible reprisals took place on the hill of Principe Pio: the general wrote to Infante Don Antonio Pascual that he had executed about 100 Spaniards. "Peasants . . . our common enemy, artisans, labourers, one or two policemen and beggars."

Almost every detail of Goya's painting is factually incorrect, but emotionally true. His firing squad fires at point-blank range; its victims are neither blindfolded or bound, and their relative statures are stage-managed to create a greater effect — if the central figure of the civilians were to stand upright he would tower over his assasins. Even the townscape, so brilliantly evocative of the spiritual paintings of El Greco, is imaginary and bears no resemblance to the actual setting of the outrage. The huge lantern that sheds its dramatic light upon the scene is a painterly invention to heighten the emotional impact of the terrible scene of secular martyrdom.

The painting is a plebeian equivalent of Jacques-Louis David's famous painting *Hommage à Marat,* but here, instead of a single figure made martyr for the people, the people themselves are commemorated, innocent victims of an individual who, like Marat, had the despotic power to make such decisions. As in David's painting, religious imagery is used to secular ends; perhaps Goya had in mind Rembrandt's spectacular use of chiaroscuro. Certainly the central figure, who looks like a Spaniard of Moorish origin, bears the hint of the stigmata on his outstretched hands, flung out as though for crucifixion. The soldiers are seen as part of an impersonal killing machine, sanctioned by the anonymity which contrasts so markedly with the individual characterization of the doomed civilians. Against the predominant black, white-yellow and ochre that makes up the basis of the painting, Goya has scrawled, dribbled and spread the unmodulated red of the blood that issues from the collapsed bodies, which lie strewn in a tragic heap at the boots of the anonymous soldiers. In a few seconds, the still-living men will join them to form an ever-growing platform for the other victims. Despite the artifice Goya has used to create the scene, the painting and its partner, which hang together in the Prado, remain an effective image of slaughter in the 19th century or today.

Goya's art provided an exciting alternative to the traditional models of painting offered to young and ambitious artists in 19th-century France. Delacroix, Manet and even the arch-Impressionist Monet admired his work. This painting was seen by the influential critic, Théophile Gautier, on his visit to Spain in 1840, and in his subsequent art criticism he was to use Goya's name frequently to denote a freedom of style and bravura technique. He claimed that Goya had made use of a spoon in the painting of this picture, and later ridiculed one of Manet's paintings, saying that "the artist appears to have taken pleasure in bringing together ignoble, low and horrible types . . . The technique calls to mind, without the verve, the most foolish of Goya's sketches when he amused himself as a painter by throwing buckets of paint at his canvases."

Goya's name became a synonym for painterly effects, and the originality of his techniques and composition left an indelible mark on avant-garde European painting which is still evident today. Manet's paintings *Olympia, The Balcony* and *The Execution of the Emperor Maximilian,* to mention only a few, are works that either directly or indirectly are inspired by Goya's example. Picasso in his 1951/2 painting *Massacre in Korea* once again used Goya's *Third of May* as the model for his own anti-war composition.

This painting, like Delacroix's *Liberty on the Barricades* or Picasso's *Guernica,* is one of the great icons of the modern age. Its dramatic force and the simplicity of its message removes it from the realm of politics to allow it to work on a humanistic level. Although painted to commemorate the savage official reprisals against the citizens of Madrid, it is more than a historical document; it is an active representation of the importance of the individual's right to life.

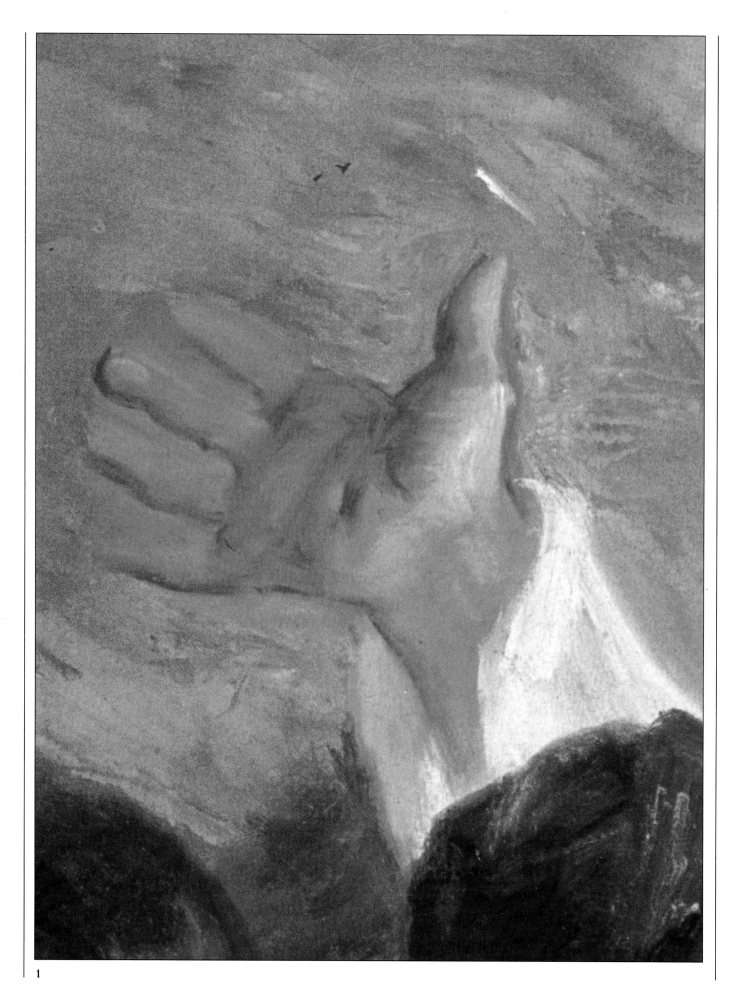

1

1 The deep indentation in the centre of the open hand suggests the stigmata — Christ's wounds caused by the nails that bore him on the cross — a religious metaphor backed up by the victim's outstretched arms. The drawing is expressive and impressionistic rather than anatomically correct, the paint has been dashed onto the canvas with great speed and assurance, the fingertips melting into the surrounding grey-blue space through which the pink ground of the canvas can be discerned. The same pink defines the bulk of the hand, while brown tones and creamy white highlights bring it into relief, a single dab of pigment on the middle finger being used to establish the roundness of it and the other fingers.

2 There is much less paint on the canvas than reproductions might lead one to expect. For all the expressive force of this painting Goya has used his paint surprisingly sparingly. The pinkish red ground is used, as so often in his work, as a positive element within the painting, and simple slabs of contrasting tone describe the forms. The handle of the sword, for example, is drawn in paint and given substance by a few stabbed-in blocks of yellow, the grey coat showing through the handle. The soldier's coats are loosely scrubbed in in grey, allowing the presence of the warm ground to modulate the tone, colour and form of the heavy garments.

2

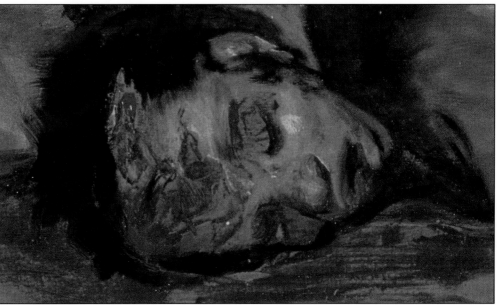

3

3 The placing of the bloodied head within the composition is significant: the painting is a large one, and the freshly slaughtered victim is uncomfortably close to the viewer's gaze as he or she stands before the canvas. The head is sketched in over the ground colour with a thin coat of grey establishing the planes, while overpainting in a lighter tone allows the ground colour to indicate the eye socket. Black is used to define both features and shadows, and red is smeared directly onto the canvas in a horrifyingly effective manner. A highlight of dirty white completes the modelling of the face.

TWO OLD PEOPLE EATING

1820-23
20³⁄₄×33¹⁄₂in/53×85cm
Oil on canvas (originally oil on plaster)
Prado, Madrid

This is one of the series of fourteen paintings Goya produced at the age of seventy-four to decorate the interior of his house, the Quinta del Sordo (the House of the Deaf Man). The name, oddly enough, refers not to Goya but to a previous occupant, also deaf. The paintings were worked directly onto the plaster of the wall, in the powerful "shorthand" style that is familiar to us from the San Antonio fresco (see page 00) and the backgrounds of Goya's smaller works. The subject matter of these works, now known as the Black Paintings, is ambiguous and often occult, and no simple thematic link between them has yet been established, although they are quite obviously meditations upon old age and the incurable folly of humanity. The subjects are nightmarish and grotesque — dark scenes from mythology, witches' sabbaths, madness and violence. This painting was the one Goya chose for his dining room. Despite — or perhaps because of — their ability to deflect the most scrupulous of scholarly research, these paintings have become some of the best known of all Goya's creations.

Thematically the individual Black Paintings refer back to ideas and images from earlier stages in Goya's *oeuvre,* his later work being an intensification of his lifelong obsession with the dark and irrational side of human life. They were painted on dark grounds and, as with the San Antonio fresco of twenty years earlier, the abiding effect, albeit on a more sombre scale, is of a vast symphonic use of grey, the colour which forms the *leitmotif* of each painting. It appears in every tone, from the palest of nuances suggestive of early morning light to total blackness, as in the background of this painting.

As always with Goya, even the simplest of pictures lend themselves to a variety of interpretations. The image of a dog up to its neck in quicksand, the painting of the two men so intent on doing each other violence that they fail to realize that they too are sinking into a bog, the Sabbat and the Pilgrimage of St Isidro are all macabre references to his earlier tapestry cartoons or his various suites of etchings. The series of his etchings entitled *Los Disparates* ("Absurdities") were produced in the same years as these works. The paintings were done entirely for his own satisfaction, and their survival is the result of a stroke of good fortune. In 1873 a German banker bought Goya's house and had the paintings transferred onto canvas. In 1878 he sent them for exhibition to Paris, where, amazingly, they passed almost without comment. Finally they were presented to the Prado Museum in 1881 where they hang together as a group to this day. Their combined effect is breathtaking. Reproductions, however good, cannot replace the experience of direct confrontation.

For whom is the mysterious repast being prepared? Are the two figures the consumers or the preparers of the food in the bowl? We do not know. The figure to the right of the old woman may be an earthly associate or — as in other works by Goya — may be a supernatural visitor of whose presence she is unaware. What is certain is that this is no simple genre scene but an image with a very personal and emblematic significance. This may be lost on the modern viewer, but we cannot but admire the masterly paint handling and expressionistic force of the work.

1 *Actual size detail*

1 *Actual size detail* This is the smallest of the Black Paintings, and shares with the others a breadth and speed of handling allied with an absolute mastery of tone. Using a very restricted palette Goya modelled his bizarre forms from a black ground, working up towards the lighter tones. The shadows and features are defined by the ground, the thick sweeps of paint creating sharp edges of richly modulated colour.

2 The Black Paintings have been much restored. Now transferred to canvas, they were originally painted *al secco*, that is, onto a dry specially prepared surface which allowed the artist to build up a considerable thickness of pigment. The surface was striated in order to receive the oil pigment, and traces of these indentations remain. However, they still convey a strong sense of spontaneity and freshness. Here powerfully modelled paint describes the sleeves, with soft highlights and touches of red and brown in the hands and bowl. The surface pattern of this area is built up with strongly defined sweeps of paint laid on with a twisting brush for dramatic effect.

3 The shrouded figure was originally much bulkier, and traces of the original silhouette can be made out above its head and shoulder. The light falling on the face is described in thick creamy paint over the dark ground. The structure of the nose is defined by leaving the black ground uncovered, whilst the impact of the eyes is strengthened with black overpainting.

2

3

Index

PHOTOGRAPHIC CREDITS
The photographs in this book were provided by the following:
Bridgeman Art Library, London 10, 12, 14 bottom, 27-29, 37-39, 45-47,
55-57; John R. Freeman & Co. Ltd, London 11 top, 13; The Frick
Collection, New York 11 bottom; Hispanic Society of America, New
York 9 bottom; Index, Barcelona 7, 8, 9 top, 15, 16 bottom, 19-21,
31-35, 49-53, 59-61; Metropolitan Museum of Art, New York 16 top,
23-25; National Gallery, London 16 centre, 41-43.